TIME FOR KIDS READERS

Where Water Comes From

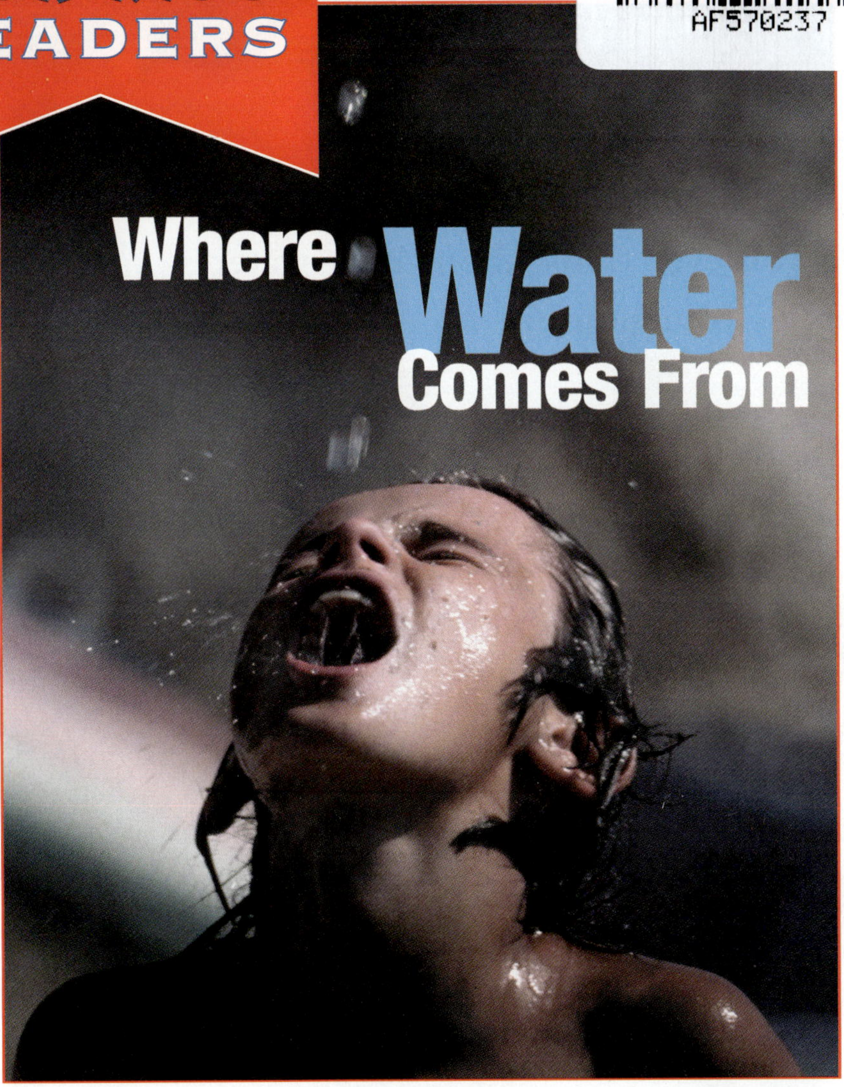

by Dan Ahearn

Harcourt

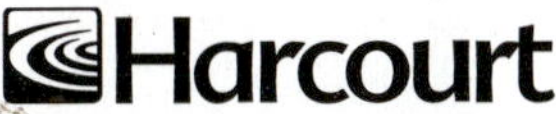

Orlando Austin Chicago New York Toronto London San Diego

Visit *The Learning Site!*
www.harcourtschool.com

Clean water comes from a faucet.

Everyone needs fresh, clean water. Do you ever think about how water gets to your house?

People used to have to carry water in jugs. This was very hard work!

In some places people still carry water in jugs. A girl in India carries a water jug on her head.

Some aqueducts are more than 2,000 years old and they are still in use.

As towns and cities began to grow, the need for large amounts of water increased. The water was far away in lakes and rivers. People needed a way to move water many miles. Long ago, the people of Rome made stone pipes to move water to their homes. These stone pipes were called *aqueducts*.

Today water comes to our homes through pipes. The pipes are buried under the ground. The first pipes in the United States were made of wood. Today they are made of concrete, metal, or plastic.

This metal water pipe was made long ago.

This river is in New Zealand.

The water in your home may start in a lake or a river. This water is full of mud and stones. The water needs to be cleaned before you can drink it.

Engineers inspect a water treatment plant.

The water is cleaned at the water treatment plant. This cleaning is done in steps. First, the water is poured into a large tank. Then, it is mixed with a substance that causes sticky clumps to form.

The clumps settle on the bottom of the tank and the cleaner water moves on. The water still needs more cleaning. In the second step, water is poured through a layer of gravel.

A machine stirs treated water so the clumps of particles fall to the bottom.

Water sits in a tank and sinks through a filter, such as sand. This removes germs and bits of dirt.

This removes any larger pieces of dirt that were missed in the first step of the process. The water then drips down through the gravel to a layer of sand. The sand removes the smallest pieces of dirt and even some germs. Now the water is fairly clean, but we're not done yet. Chlorine is added to kill any germs that are left. Fluoride is also added. Fluoride helps protect your teeth. Now the clean water is ready to go to town. It flows through a very large pipe until it gets to the city.

Treated water flows through large pipes to towns and cities.

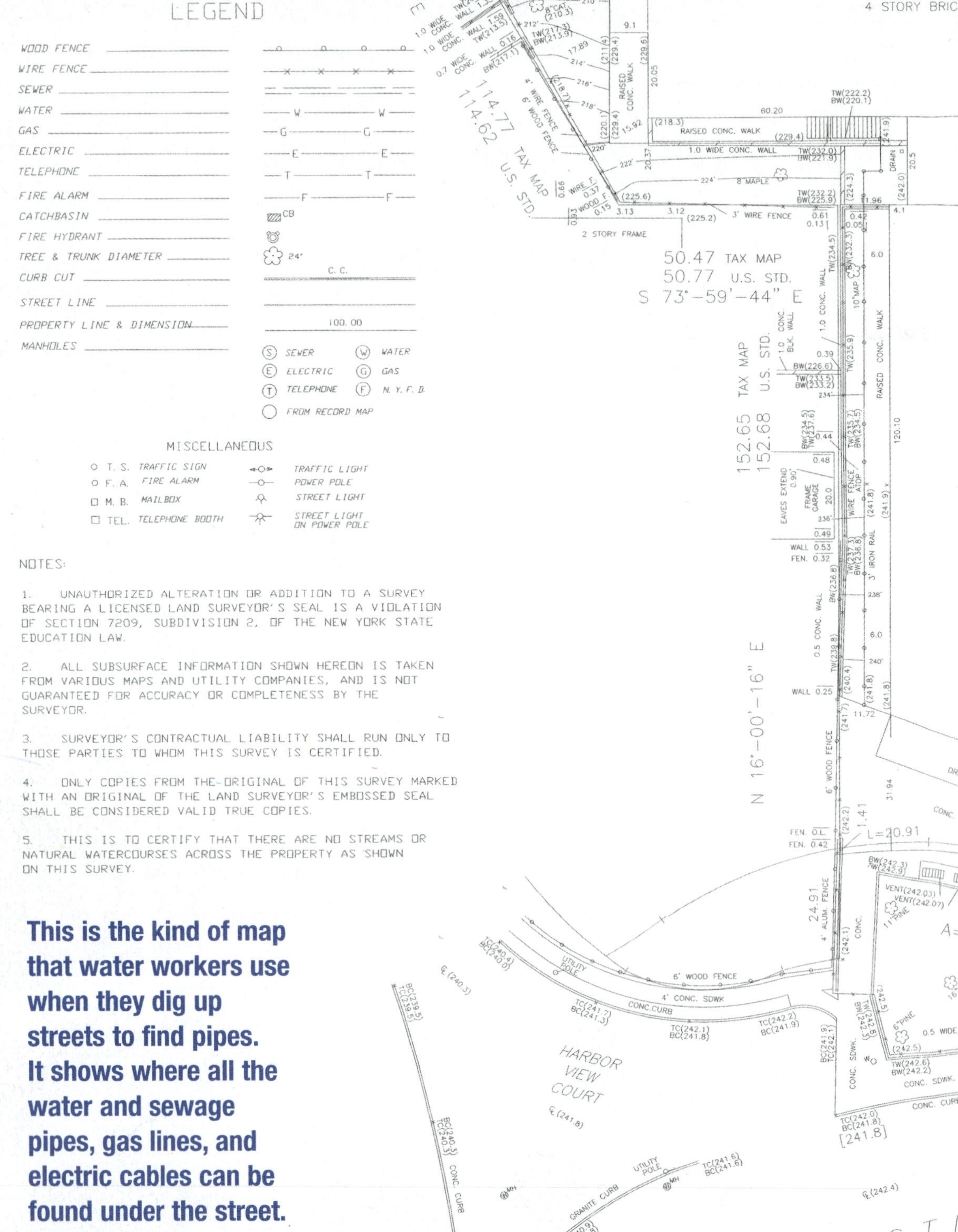

This is the kind of map that water workers use when they dig up streets to find pipes. It shows where all the water and sewage pipes, gas lines, and electric cables can be found under the street.

This man is installing the water pipes for a new house.

In the city, the water goes into pipes called water mains. Water mains travel under the street. They carry water all over town. From the mains, water flows into smaller pipes connected to buildings. Inside your house, for example, even smaller pipes go to the kitchen and the bathroom.

The force that moves the water on its journey is called water pressure. Water pressure can lift the water straight up the side of a building. It's very strong.

Water travels a long distance before falling from your faucet.

It's a big job getting water to your house. Water has to be collected and cleaned at a water plant. Then it must travel through miles and miles of pipe.

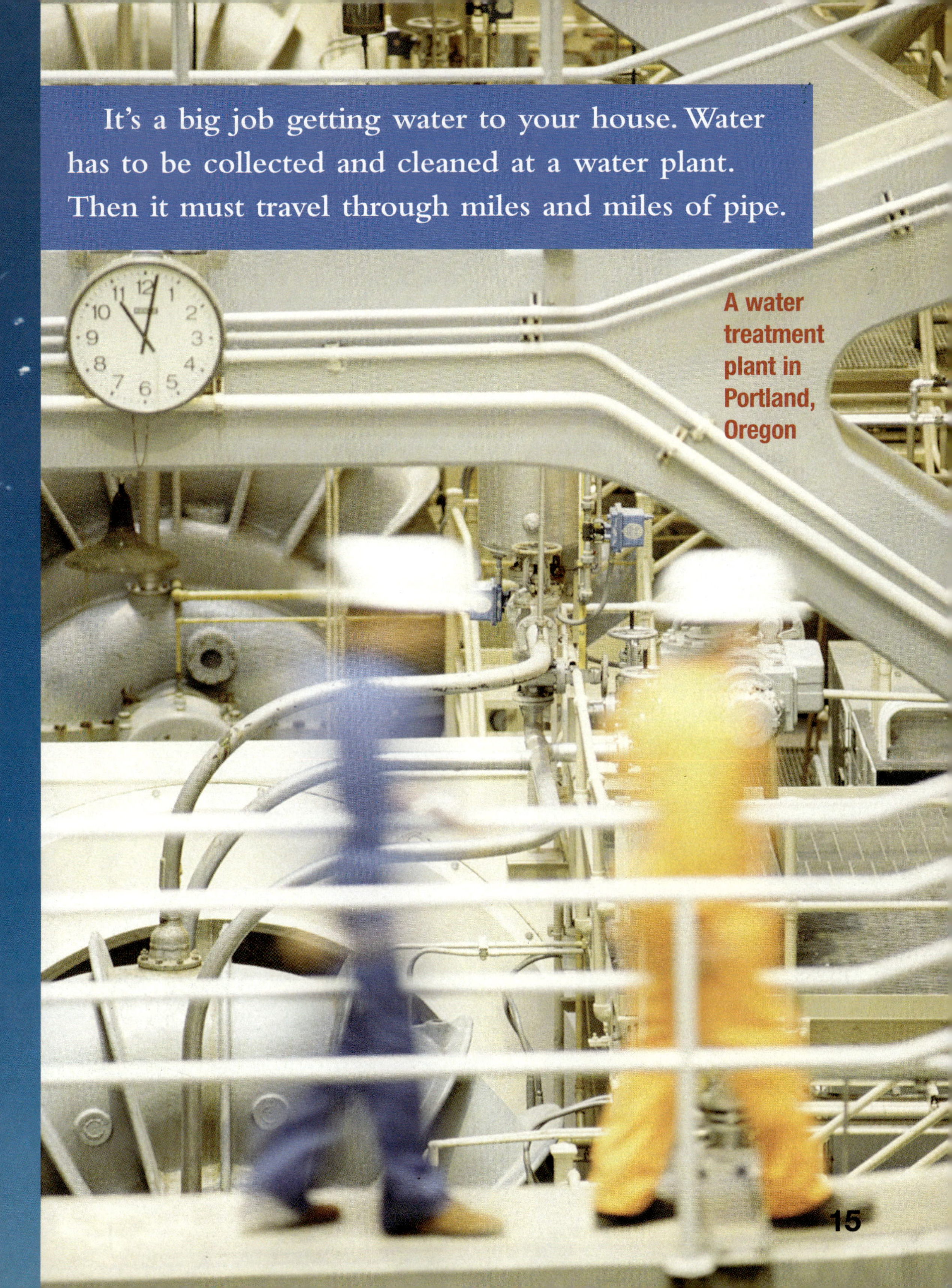

A water treatment plant in Portland, Oregon

A city's water department hires many people to keep the water running. You have a lot of people to thank for that glass of water. Thanks to them, all you have to do is turn the faucet and out it comes. Simple!

It takes many people to bring you clean water.